The Simple Slow Cooker Recipe Book

Delicious Slow Cooked Meals for the Whole Family Complete With Full Recipe Lists

Lucy Bucker

ISBN - 9798351664064

Table of Contents

Introduction 7

What Is A Slow Cooker? 8

How Should You Use A Slow Cooker? 8

What Maintenance Is Involved? 10

What Are The Advantages Of Using A Slow Cooker? 11

Tips & Tricks For Making The Most Of Your Slow Cooker 14

What Problems You Might Encounter With Your Slow Cooker 18

Great Slow Cooker Breakfast Recipes 21

Slow Cooker Oatmeal 22

Slow Cooker Veggie And Eggs 25

Slow Cooker French Toast With Blueberry Syrup 29

Slow Cooker Banana Bread 34

Slow Cooker Frittata Omelette 38

Healthy Lunch Recipes 43

Chicken Soup In A Slow Cooker 44

Tomato Soup With Crème Fraîche 48

Slow Cooker Mac And Cheese 52

Slow Cooker Pizza Recipe 56

Cheesy Potato Bake 60

Vegetarian Tortilla Lasagna 64

Amazing Slow Cooker Dinner Recipes 69

Beef And Broccoli 70

Slow Cooker Spaghetti Bolognese 74

Slow Cooked Lemon And Salmon 79

Slow Cooker Sweet Potatoes Wedges 82

Slow Cooker Ratatouille 84

Slow Cooker Pork Roast 88

Stuffed Peppers In The Slow Cooker 92

Garlic Mushrooms 96

Autumnal Vegetable Soup...100

Conclusion...104

Disclaimer...108

EXCLUSIVE BONUS

40 Weight Loss Recipes

&

14 Days Meal Plan

Scan the QR-Code and receive
the FREE download:

Introduction

Have you recently bought or been gifted a slow cooker? This amazing piece of kit is a perfect way to transform your cooking experience and the way in which you organize your life, but it's important to learn how to use it effectively so that you are getting the most from it. You can't just toss ingredients in and hope for the best; there's a little more to it than that. In this book, we're going to look at how to use and maintain your slow cooker, some of the top advantages that it offers, and – of course – amazing, healthy recipes to ensure your slow cooker is doing what you need.

Slow cookers are often used to make tough cuts of meat more tender and juicy, but you don't have to confine yourself to exclusively meat. There are plenty of vegetarian and vegan dishes that work well in a slow cooker too! The more range you have, the more use you will get from your slow cooker, and the more money you'll shave off your energy bills.

What Is A Slow Cooker?

Commonly called a crock-pot, a slow cooker is an electric-powered kitchen gadget that is designed to come to a low temperature and stay there for an extended period in order to cook food. The cooker usually has a highly insulated pan, and is heated slowly from underneath. The heat permeates through the slow cooker and its contents, gradually warming them, and the insulation minimizes how much of this heat is lost to the surrounding air.

A slow cooker is usually plugged in and operates on a counter, and it is designed to be run for several hours at a time. In general, it is intended to replace boiling, rather than other cooking methods (e.g. frying, roasting), and the food it results in is more like boiled foods. Many people find that their slow cooker is particularly good for stews and soups, but it can make plenty of other meals as well. Don't be afraid to experiment and try out new recipes; your family may love them.

How Should You Use A Slow Cooker?

A slow cooker is great to use when you are going to be out of the house, or when you'll be around but you don't want to be standing in the kitchen for hours at a time. You can switch it on, forget about it, and come back later to find a hot meal waiting for you.

Indeed, you don't want to be checking on your slow cooker constantly, because taking the lid off will slow down the cooking process. It's okay to remove the lid when you need to (e.g. for adding ingredients), but you should not be lifting it off for other reasons. It lets heat escape from the cooker, and this means your food will take noticeably longer to cook.

You should therefore use a slow cooker for a hands-off cooking style where you can put some food on in the morning and forget about it until late afternoon or evening. With the right recipe, you may be able to leave your slow cooker unattended for a full workday, meaning that you can set it going in the morning and come home to a delicious, hot meal already waiting – and minimal clean-up.

You can cook some of your standard recipes in a slow cooker too, although you'll have to figure out the timing. As a very rough estimate, 15-30 minutes on a traditional cooker translates to 1-2 hours on high in the slow cooker, or 4-6 hours on low. 1-2 hours on the traditional cooker equals 3-4 hours on high or 6-8 hours on low. It's important to test different recipes out and measure how long they take, however, as this is only a rule of thumb, and not a fixed guide.

What Maintenance Is Involved?

You will need to look after your slow cooker well if you want it to last. Slow cookers can be expensive items, so you want to make sure that you don't do anything that will ruin its glaze or ability to hold onto heat.

You should wash your slow cooker after every use, but this must be done with care. The slow cooker should be completely cool before you put it in water. Some slow cookers can be placed in the dishwasher, but many need to be hand-washed in the sink.

Make sure that you use a soft sponge, and never put abrasive cleaners or scourers on your slow cooker. Hot water and soap should be enough to free any stuck food. Because a slow cooker doesn't reach very high temperatures, food will usually come off with a gentle scrub, and shouldn't need scouring. If any food has got stuck, allow it to soak in warm water for a while, and then give it another rub. It should come off.

Never immerse your slow cooker in water, however. The base of the cooker will absorb liquid and this could ruin it when you next use it to cook. A small splash shouldn't be a problem, but you need to make sure that the underside of the slow cooker stays dry and is never left standing in water.

If the electric part of your slow cooker gets dirty, use a damp, soapy cloth to wipe it clean, but do not put this part in or near water.

What Are The Advantages Of Using A Slow Cooker?

So, if slow cookers are so fiddly to look after, you may be wondering whether you truly want to use one – but the benefits certainly outweigh the disadvantages with these clever gadgets, so let's explore what those are.

Firstly, slow cookers help the nutrients in the food to remain more stable. Because it never heats past a certain point, a slow cooker doesn't break down the food to the same degree as other cooking methods, and this may help to trap more nutrition in the food, making it better for you.

Additionally, any nutrients that do come out in the steam will be caught on the lid, and will run back into the liquid below. This results in them being returned to the meal, meaning that you lose very little nutrition when you cook with one of these gadgets, and ensuring you get the best from your food.

Secondly, a major advantage is that you can leave a slow cooker unattended. These units are intended to be safe even when left on for hours without being checked, and many people who have packed schedules use them to make their workdays easier and ensure that they still have healthy food to come back to. It can be a hassle to cook when you've been at work for hours, and if you often find yourself succumbing to the temptation of takeaways and fast food or microwave meals, you may find a slow cooker is the answer.

You can prepare your food in advance, leave it cooking all day, and come home to a waiting dinner. There will also be minimal clean-up left to do, and you'll have effectively made the healthy option the easier choice – which is a great way to ensure that you take it. Slow cookers are perfect for people who are too busy to cook every day. Even if you work from home, you can benefit from using one, as you won't have to constantly jump up to check on the pot you've got simmering on the stove.

Next, slow cookers are useful because they help to reduce costs. A slow cooker lets you make the most of the tough cuts of meat, which tend to be the most economical options. The long cooking process will help to break down the meats and make them tender and delicious. This can also work well with tough vegetables, meaning you can make use of rooty options that may not be so palatable if they aren't cooked for a long time.

Slow cookers also help the flavours to meld together well, ensuring that the dish absorbs the herbs and spices. Furthermore, using one keeps your kitchen cooler, which is great when you don't fancy cooking in the summer. This can make a big difference to how hot your home gets, especially if you spend most of the day at home. It may save you from having to resort to fans and air conditioners.

Using a slow cooker will also save electricity because they use so little at a time, and this will result in a lower electricity bill overall. If you do a lot of cooking, especially of meals that take a long time (e.g. dried beans), a slow cooker could make a big impact on how much you are paying by the month. This is especially true if you are billed according to the time of day and you can leave the slow cooker on overnight.

Finally, slow cooking is a great way to cut down on your oil and fat intake. Because of the low temperatures involved, little or no oil should be needed for a recipe, which means you can reduce how much you eat dramatically, especially if you were depending on a lot of fried foods prior to getting a slow cooker. Ditch the fried eggs, tomatoes, chips, and bacon, and start making yourself some satisfying meals from scratch, without the oil!

Tips & Tricks For Making The Most Of Your Slow Cooker

Here are a few tips that you might find useful when you first starting using your slow cooker.

- Make use of herbs and spices. These bring out the flavour in all meals, but with a slow cooker, they are crucial. They will have the opportunity to really cook in and can make your meals shine. Warm spices are particularly good in a slow cooker, so opt for things like rosemary, turmeric, cumin, cayenne pepper, paprika, and black pepper. These will enrich your foods, especially if you use the fresh version of these herbs where you can. It's also thought that some of these spices will improve your digestion and can boost your circulation, so don't be afraid to start using them in your recipes!

- Trim off the excess fat from meat. As mentioned, very little (if any) fat is needed in a slow cooker, so you can remove this from the cuts before you cook them. As long as there is adequate moisture in the slow cooker, there's no risk of the food burning, so take a sharp knife and trim away any unnecessary fat on the meat before you cook it. You might think that you would rather leave the fat on, but it's important to note that when you fry fatty meat, most of it melts off and is discarded – but that won't be the case in a slow cooker. The fat will stay in the meal, and can make it greasy and heavy. If you don't want pools of oil in your food, trim off the fat and enjoy a healthier diet!

❧ Use flour if you need to thicken the food. If you're used to cooking on a stove, you may find that your meals initially come out rather thin when using the slow cooker. This is because traditional cooking methods result in a lot of water being lost as steam, but the slow cooker's lid traps this and incorporates it back into the meal, so be aware of this potential issue. If you find you're having a problem, stir a little flour fried in butter into your meal and allow it to bubble and thicken for a few minutes. You can also add less liquid or more vegetables to adjust the ratios as you become more familiar with the slow cooker.

❧ Practice your recipes first. Using a slow cooker does involve slightly different techniques, so you may find it helps to try out your recipes when you are at home to correct if they are getting too dry, staying too wet, or running into other issues. This can prevent a meal from going wrong while you aren't around to rescue it. It's also worth noting that cooking times can vary significantly between slow cookers. Although the best efforts are made to give accurate estimates for cooking times, make sure you test these for yourself and adjust recipes accordingly.

◄ Add your ingredients all at once (in general). Because the slow cooker works based on trapping heat in effectively, it's important not to keep removing the lid, so you don't want to be constantly adding ingredients once you have started the cooking process. However, it is important to be aware that some recipes will call for an ingredient or two to be added later, and this can make the dish nicer – so this isn't a hard and fast rule that must be followed at all times.

◄ Prep the ingredients in advance. If you find you're constantly rushing in the morning and it's a struggle to get the food into the slow cooker before you rush off to work, consider just chopping them the night before. You can then get the ingredients out of the fridge when you get up, preheat your slow cooker, and toss the ingredients in when they reach room temperature. Note that they don't have to be at room temperature when they hit the slow cooker, but this often results in food that tastes better, so it's a good idea to give them a bit of time to warm up before adding them if they've been in the fridge. Almost all ingredients can be prepared in advance so that you minimize what you need to do in the morning. Breaking meal prep up into steps like this may also make it a less daunting task.

❧ Look for simple recipes where you can. The point of the slow cooker is to reduce the amount of hassle that you face, and you should avoid recipes that require you to spend hours preparing vegetables and meats before you even add them to the slow cooker. It's true that frying onions first and occasionally browning the meat will improve the flavour of the final dish, but this isn't crucial in most cases, and you should generally try to choose recipes that are going to be straightforward and save you time.

❧ Make sure your slow cooker is filled to the correct level. It generally wants to be between half full and two-thirds full, as this ensures that it is safe and cooking efficiently. Don't operate your slow cooker if it is very close to empty.

❧ If your recipe includes dairy, add it at the end, when there is half an hour or less of cooking time remaining. This will ensure that it retains its texture and doesn't get overheated, which might cause it to coagulate in the cooker. In almost every case, dairy only needs to be warmed to taste great in your dish, and 30 minutes should provide plenty of time for it to melt or cook in.

What Problems You Might Encounter With Your Slow Cooker

Of course, no cooking method is perfect, and slow cookers can cause a few issues at times. Let's explore what pitfalls you might hit and how to avoid them.

- Your meat has come out tough, in spite of a long cooking time. This usually happens if you've cooked very lean meat, which tends to dry out when it is over-cooked. Choose plumper cuts, or leave a little bit of the fat on to help reduce the drying effect. Alternatively, reduce the cooking time. As a rough rule of thumb, you should be cooking meat for about an hour and a half per pound (on low) or a bit less. If you cook the meat for too long, it will become dry and tough.

- There's no automatic shut-off. This is a big annoyance with many slow cookers. If your recipe says the food needs six hours on low and you're at work for eight hours, you're going to be faced with an over-cooked meal, or the recipe is simply off the menu. However, you can get around this issue by adding a timer to your plug socket and making sure the slow cooker will turn itself off automatically when it's done.

- The food isn't cooking evenly. This can be an issue if you are adding both tough ingredients (e.g. carrots) and soft ones (e.g. peas). The best way to get around this is to add any soft, fast-cooking ingredients at the end of the cooking time, rather than the start. This can still fit nicely into a workday. If you add things like peas as soon as you get in from work, you can change, have a cup of tea, and set the table while the meal finishes cooking, and your ingredients will all be cooked to perfection. You don't have to put everything in the cooker before you leave the house.

- It makes too much. This is one of the biggest pitfalls that slow cookers suffer from; they can be hard for small households to deal with. They should be at least half full, or the food will end up overcooked, but what should you do if you end up with lots of leftovers? The answer is to either get a smaller slow cooker, or to get into the habit of bulk cooking and freezing. This can be a great way to reduce your workload throughout the week; you can just grab a container of delicious stew from your freezer before leaving for work and let it thaw in the fridge – ready for you when you get home!

So, with all that in mind, let's now get on to some great slow cooker recipes that you can make at home.

EXCLUSIVE BONUS

40 Weight Loss Recipes

&

14 Days Meal Plan

Scan the QR-Code and receive
the FREE download:

Great Slow Cooker Breakfast Recipes

You might not often think about using your slow cooker to make breakfast, but it's perfect for doing so, and all you need to do is add the ingredients and set it going the night before to ensure that you wake up to a piping hot cooked breakfast. This is perfect for weekends when you want to be lazy but you also want to enjoy something delicious and hot before you start the day!

Slow Cooker Oatmeal

Do you love oatmeal in the morning? With a timer switch, you can come down to oatmeal ready and waiting, getting a superbly healthy start to the day.

Serves: 4

You will need:

- ♦ 80 g / 1 cup of oats
- ♦ 80 g / 0.5 cups of raisins
- ♦ 470 ml / 2 cups of whole milk
- ♦ 1 peeled apple (preferably tart but you can use a sweet one)
- ♦ 50 g / ¼ cup of brown sugar
- ♦ 25 g / ¼ cup of walnuts (chopped)
- ♦ ¼ teaspoon of salt
- ♦ 1/3 teaspoon of ground cinnamon
- ♦ 1 tablespoon of butter (melted)

Method:

1. Melt the butter.

2. Add all of the ingredients to the slow cooker and cook on low for approximately 3 and a half hours, until the milk has been fully soaked up and the oats have become tender. You can use a timer for this if you want to make the recipe overnight.

3. Serve with an extra sprinkling of brown sugar, some cream, a few raspberries, extra walnuts, or any other toppings that you enjoy. The rest of the oatmeal can be stored in the fridge and heated up on later days if you don't finish it on that day.

Nutritional info:

Calories: 329

Fat: 12.9 g

Cholesterol: 20 mg

Sodium: 222 mg

Carbohydrates: 47.7 g

Fibre: 3.8 g

Protein: 9.2 g

Slow Cooker Veggie And Eggs

If you love eggs in the morning, you don't have to get up and fry them first thing; this vegetable and egg breakfast combo is a great slow cooker option that you can make the night before, and it tastes fantastic. It's also a healthy way to start the day, getting some of your five vegetables in straight away.

Serves: 8

You will need:

- 60 g / 1 cup mushrooms (sliced, fresh)
- 1 green pepper (chopped)
- 280 g / 10 oz frozen spinach (thawed and squeezed until dry)
- 1 medium onion (peeled and chopped into fine slices)
- 230 ml / 1 cup of 2% milk
- 230 ml / 1 cup of water
- 8 eggs (large)
- 1.8 kg / 4 lb. of potatoes (peeled and sliced thinly)
- 240 g / 2 cups of cheddar cheese (grated)
- ½ teaspoon of pepper
- 1½ teaspoons of salt

Method:

4. Warm your slow cooker and add a small amount of oil at the bottom (this recipe has little water in it). Wipe the oil around the slow cooker to coat the bottom, ensuring that the ingredients don't burn.

5. Peel the potatoes and onions and chop them into fine slices.

6. Wash the mushrooms and chop them into fine slices.

7. Wash and chop the pepper, removing the seeds.

8. Squeeze out the spinach to remove the excess water.

9. Grate the cheese.

10. Layer the potatoes, green pepper, spinach, mushrooms, and onion in the bottom of the slow cooker, alternating between ingredients to get a good distribution.

11. In a large bowl, whisk together the eggs, water, milk, salt, and pepper, plus any other seasoning that you fancy. Once the mixture is frothy, pour it over the top of the vegetables in the slow cooker.

12. Sprinkle the grated cheese across the top, add the lid, and cook on low for about 8 hours. The potatoes should be tender and the eggs fully set before you serve this meal.

Nutritional info:

Calories: 376

Fat: 15.4 g

Cholesterol: 218 mg

Sodium: 595 mg

Carbohydrates: 41.5 g

Fibre: 6.9 g

Protein: 19.7 g

Slow Cooker French Toast With Blueberry Syrup

If you love a decadent breakfast with some fruit on the side, this French toast is the perfect option for you. It's sweet enough to make a fantastic weekend treat, but it does incorporate blueberries, which are a great option for kids and adults alike. It's a bit more involved than some of the other slow cooker recipes, but that makes it perfect for celebrations. It does require you to cook it on the day, however, so you'll need to work out your timing and how it can be slotted into your normal routine.

Serves: 12

You will need:

♦ 200 g / 1 cup of sugar

♦ 240 ml / 1 cup of cold water

♦ 2 tablespoons of cornflour / cornstarch

♦ 1 tablespoon of butter

- ◆ 140 g / ¾ cup of blueberries
- ◆ 1 tablespoon of lemon juice

For the French toast:

- ◆ 340 g / 12 oz cream cheese (cut into cubes)
- ◆ ½ teaspoon of ground cinnamon
- ◆ 240 ml / 1 cup of 2% milk
- ◆ 80 ml / 1/3 cup of maple syrup
- ◆ 1 teaspoon of vanilla extract
- ◆ 80 ml / 1/3 cup of sour cream
- ◆ 120 ml / ½ cup of plain yoghurt
- ◆ 8 eggs (large)
- ◆ 450 g / 1 lb French bread (cut into cubes)
- ◆ 285 g / 1½ cups of blueberries

Note: you can use frozen blueberries or fresh ones for both the syrup and the main recipe, and it should work fine.

Method:

1. Take out a large mixing bowl and crack in the eggs. Add the sour cream, cinnamon, vanilla, and yoghurt, and then whisk together well.

2. Add the milk and maple syrup to the bowl and whisk until fully combined.

3. Cut the French bread into cubes and separate half of it out. Layer this at the bottom of your slow cooker, and then rinse the blueberries and add half of them on top of the bread.

4. Cut your cream cheese into cubes and add half on top, and then pour half of the egg mixture over this.

5. Repeat the layers, starting with the French bread, followed by the blueberries, cream cheese, and egg mixture.

6. Once you have finished, place your slow cooker vessel in the fridge and put the lid on. Refrigerate it for the whole night, and then take it out about 30 minutes before you intend to start cooking. Leave it on the counter to warm. It's important to follow this step, as it gives time for the egg to soak into the bread and makes the resulting toast rich and fluffy.

7. Once the vessel has warmed up, cook the French toast on low for approximately 3 ½ hours, or until a knife comes out clean.

8. While the French toast is cooking, make the blueberry syrup. Get a small saucepan and mix together your sugar and cornstarch. Stir water into the mixture until it has become smooth, and then stir in about a third of your blueberries, reserving the rest.

9. Bring this to a boil, constantly stirring so that it doesn't stick. It should take about three minutes for the berries to begin swelling and bursting. When they do, keep stirring for a few more minutes, and then remove it from the heat, and stir in your lemon juice, butter, and the berries that you reserved. This syrup can then be poured over the warm French toast to make a truly delicious and decadent breakfast. Note that it's best served straight away, so time your cooking carefully.

Nutritional info:

Calories: 399

Fat: 16.8 g

Cholesterol: 164 mg

Sodium: 405 mg

Carbohydrates: 51.3 g

Fibre: 1.5 g

Protein: 12.4 g

Slow Cooker Banana Bread

Many people find fruit and sweet breads are the easiest things to stomach in the morning, and if that's the case for you, you'll love this banana bread. It's a straightforward recipe that will make you a deliciously moist loaf to enjoy, warm or cold, toasted or not, when you first wake up. Save yourself some really ripe bananas for this, as it works best when the bananas are black.

Note that for this recipe, you will need a bread pan that fits into your slow cooker. If it sits right at the base, you will also need a rack so it doesn't touch the ceramic. If it doesn't, you shouldn't need a rack. If it does sit at the bottom and you haven't got a rack, add about 120 ml / ½ cup of water to the bottom, making sure you don't splash the banana bread. This will stop the pan from overheating.

> Serves: 1 loaf (approximately 10 slices)

You will need:

- ♦ ¹/₂ teaspoon of salt

- ♦ 2 eggs (beaten)

- ♦ 3 medium bananas (mashed)

- ♦ ¹/₂ teaspoon of bicarbonate of soda / baking soda

- ♦ 1 teaspoon of baking powder

- ♦ ¹/₂ teaspoon of salt

- ♦ 75 g / 1/3 cup of butter (softened)

- ♦ 100 g / ¹/₂ cup sugar

- ♦ 50 g / ¹/₂ cup of walnuts (chopped)

- ♦ 225 g / 1 ³/₄ cups of plain / all-purpose flour

Method:

1. Get out a large mixing bowl and add the soft butter and your sugar. Beat well until fluffy and fully mixed.

2. Get out a second bowl and sift together the salt, flour, bicarbonate of soda / baking soda, and baking powder.

3. Peel and mash your ripe bananas thoroughly.

4. Add a little ripe banana and then a little of the flour mixture to the sugar and butter and mix well. Keep doing this, alternating between banana and flour, until you have mixed everything together and it is fully combined.

5. Chop your walnuts, and then sprinkle them into your batter and mix them in.

6. Grease a loaf pan and then pour the batter into it and place it in the slow cooker (see notes about this at the start of the recipe).

7. Carefully fold up some paper towels and place them over the top of the loaf pan. This will prevent the lid of the slow cooker from dripping water onto your banana bread and ruining it.

8. Put the lid on the slow cooker and turn the cooker to high. Cook for up to 3 hours, and then insert a toothpick into the centre. If it comes out clean, the loaf is ready, but if the batter is still wet, give it a bit longer. This should ensure your loaf is deliciously cooked.

Nutritional info (based on one slice if you cut the loaf into 10):

Calories: 236

Fat: 11 g

Cholesterol: 49 mg

Sodium: 236 mg

Carbohydrates: 31.1 g

Fibre: 1.4 g

Protein: 5.1 g

Slow Cooker Frittata Omelette

Do you love omelettes? If you do but they seem a bit more effort than they are worth when it comes to getting out of bed, try this slow cooker omelette instead. It's also great for an easy supper if you've got a particularly busy day, so it doesn't have to be reserved for breakfasts only.

Note: you need a rack and a baking dish that will fit into your slow cooker for this recipe.

You will need:

- 1 onion (sliced)
- 12 eggs (large)
- 1 medium potato (peeled and sliced)
- 1 tablespoon of olive oil
- ½ teaspoon of salt
- Pinch of pepper
- 1 teaspoon of hot pepper sauce (or similar sauce)
- 75 g / ½ cup of green pepper (chopped)
- 225 / ½ pound of deli ham (chopped)
- 120 g / 1 cup of cheddar cheese (grated)

Method:

1. Peel and slice your onion and potato, aiming for fine slices so that they will cook quickly.

2. Wash and chop your green pepper, removing the seeds.

3. Chop the deli ham.

4. Grate the cheddar cheese.

5. Heat some oil in a large skillet over a medium heat, and then add the onion and potato. Cook for approximately 5 minutes, until the potato is starting to turn golden.

6. Tip this mixture into a greased baking dish and set it aside.

7. Get a large mixing bowl and add the eggs. Whisk them and add the salt, pepper, and pepper sauce until you have a smooth and frothy mixture. Stir in half of the cheese, plus the green pepper and ham.

8. Pour this mixture over the potato and onion mixture, and then sprinkle the rest of the cheese on top.

9. Place the dish on the rack in your slow cooker and put the lid on. Set the slow cooker to low and cook for approximately 3 ½ hours. Once the eggs have set, insert a knife into the centre and check that it comes out clean before serving the meal.

Nutritional info:

Calories: 334

Fat: 21.8 g

Cholesterol: 413 mg

Sodium: 947 mg

Carbohydrates: 10.2 g

Fibre: 1.7 g

Protein: 24.5 g

Healthy Lunch Recipes

Of course, slow cookers tend to be used for making lunches and dinners, and there are some great recipes that you can create here too. Whenever you want a hot lunch, your slow cooker is an ideal way to ensure that you don't spend your whole morning in the kitchen.

Chicken Soup In A Slow Cooker

Chicken soup is a staple in many households. It makes a great light lunch, and it's an easy, nutritious meal that many people love. Fortunately, it's also easy to make in a slow cooker, and the preparation should only take about fifteen minutes in total. You can easily scale the batch up so that you have some for freezing, too.

Serves: 7

You will need:

- ♦ 680 g / 1½ lb. of chicken breast (boneless, skinned)
- ♦ The juice from one lemon
- ♦ Two leeks (sliced)
- ♦ 3 celery sticks (chopped)
- ♦ 1 onion (chopped)
- ♦ 3 carrots (chopped)
- ♦ 2 bay leaves
- ♦ ½ teaspoon of thyme (dried)
- ♦ ½ teaspoon of rosemary (dried)
- ♦ 2 tablespoons of parsley (chopped)
- ♦ 2 l / 8 ½ cups of chicken stock
- ♦ 4 cloves of garlic (minced)
- ♦ 225 g / 8 oz spaghetti (break into thirds)
- ♦ Salt and pepper to taste

Method:

1. Start by peeling and chopping your onion, dicing it finely.

2. Wash the leeks and halve them, and then slice the halves into fine shreds.

3. Wash and dice the celery sticks and carrots.

4. Juice the lemon and crush the garlic. Chop any fresh herbs.

5. Break your spaghetti noodles into rough thirds.

6. Season the chicken with salt and pepper, and any other flavourings you enjoy.

7. Place the chicken into your slow cooker, and pour some chicken stock in too. Stir in your celery, carrots, onion, garlic, herbs, and bay leaves. Season lightly, and then turn the slow cooker on to a low heat and cook for up to eight hours.

8. As the soup finishes cooking, remove the lid from the slow cooker, take the chicken out, and shred it thoroughly.

9. Stir the chicken back into the soup, followed by the pasta. Mix well, put the lid back on, and continue to cook on low until the pasta is tender. This should take around half an hour, or a little longer.

10. Check that the pasta is soft enough to eat, and then mix in the lemon juice and parsley, and serve the soup piping hot. It's delicious with crusty bread in particular.

Nutritional info:

Calories: 219

Fat: 6.1 g

Cholesterol: 77 mg

Sodium: 710 mg

Carbohydrates: 16.7 g

Fibre: 0.9 g

Protein: 23.3 g

Tomato Soup With Crème Fraîche

Tomato soup is one of the most popular options out there. It's rich, flavourful, healthy, vegetarian, and very warming on a cold day. Whip up a batch of tomato soup and you'll have lunches for the week! You can leave the crème fraîche out of this recipe if you want to make a vegan version (and swap the butter for oil), or you can leave it in for a creamy, richer version. Either way, it will taste delicious!

You will need:

- 1kg 50 g / 2lb. 5 oz of fresh tomatoes (chopped)

- 3 cloves of garlic (minced)

- 40 g / 1 ½ oz of butter

- 1 onion (chopped)

- 15 g / ½ oz fresh basil (chopped)

- 3 tablespoons of tomato puree

- 3 tablespoons of crème fraîche

- 400 ml / 14 fl oz of vegetable stock

Method:

1. Wash the basil well, pick the leaves off the stalks, and put the leaves in a bowl to one side for later use. Chop your stalks up small and then add the pieces to the slow cooker.

2. Wash and chop your tomatoes into rough chunks.

3. Peel and chop the onion and the garlic, and mince the basil leaves.

4. Tip all of the ingredients except for the crème fraîche into the slow cooker, and stir so that they are evenly distributed across the bottom of the vessel.

5. Turn the slow cooker on to high, put the lid on, and cook for 3 hours. Stab a tomato with a fork to check that it is tender, and cook for longer if it still feels firm.

6. Stir in the crème fraîche and the basil leaves, and then transfer the soup to a blender. You may need to do this a little at a time, depending on the size of your blender and the amount of soup that you have made.

7. Blend the soup thoroughly, until it is completely smooth. You may need to add a little water or vegetable stock if the soup is too thick, but it should be close to the right consistency. Taste and then add seasoning, and serve piping hot with crusty bread.

Nutritional info:

Calories: 189

Fat: 13.3 g

Cholesterol: 22 mg

Sodium:86 mg

Carbohydrates: 16.5 g

Fibre: 4.4 g

Protein: 3.6 g

Slow Cooker Mac And Cheese

Who doesn't love a big bowlful of mac and cheese? This dish is super tasty, and makes a wonderful lunch for kids and for adults. It's also very easy to toss into a slow cooker, and you can add other cheeses to change the flavour if you like, or include some Greek yoghurt to cut down on the fat if you prefer. Leftovers will store well in the fridge, or in an airtight container in the freezer, making easy meals for later in the week!

Serves: 9

You will need:

- ♦ 450 g / 1 lb. macaroni
- ♦ 480 g / 4 cups of cheddar cheese (grated)
- ♦ 60 g / ½ cup of Parmesan (grated)
- ♦ ¼ teaspoon of paprika
- ♦ 115 g / ½ cup of melted butter
- ♦ 470 ml / 2 cups of whole milk
- ♦ 1 garlic clove (crushed)
- ♦ 700 ml / 24 oz of evaporated milk
- ♦ 115 g / 4 oz of cream cheese
- ♦ Pinch of salt
- ♦ Pinch of pepper
- ♦ Handful of chives (chopped, optional)

Method:

1. Peel and crush the garlic, and grate the Parmesan and cheddar cheese. Melt the butter.

2. Add the butter, cheddar cheese, Parmesan, macaroni, cream cheese, garlic clove, paprika, milk, and evaporated milk to the slow cooker. Season with pepper and salt, or add other spices if you prefer.

3. Put the lid on and turn the slow cooker on to high, and then cook until the sauce has become thick and rich and the pasta has cooked fully. This should take about 2 ½ hours, but you should start checking at the 2 hour mark and take it out sooner if necessary.

4. Chop the chives finely and then serve the pasta with a sprinkling of chives on top. Cool any leftovers and store them in an airtight container in the fridge or freezer.

Nutritional info:

Calories: 680

Fat: 40.9 g

Cholesterol: 126 mg

Sodium: 604 mg

Carbohydrates: 49.1 g

Fibre: 1.6 g

Protein: 29.2 g

Slow Cooker Pizza Recipe

It's probably never occurred to you that you can make a pizza in your slow cooker, but you can! This is a great way to get a freshly baked pizza without having to have your oven on for hours, and it's easy to adapt this recipe to suit your tastes. Make a vegetarian version by removing the pepperoni and swapping in olives or some crispy vegetables or extra cheese. This makes a fantastic lunch!

Serves: 3

You will need:

- ♦ Cooking spray
- ♦ 225 g / 1 cup of pizza sauce
- ♦ 60 g / ½ cup of Parmesan (grated)
- ♦ 70 g / ½ cup of pepperoni (sliced)
- ♦ 450 g / 1 lb. of pizza dough
- ♦ ½ teaspoon of Italian seasoning
- ♦ 1 teaspoon of fresh parsley (chopped)
- ♦ Pinch of crushed red pepper flakes
- ♦ 450 g / 2 cups of mozzarella (grated)

Method:

1. Carefully spray your slow cooker with a little oil, lining the bottom and sides. If you don't have cooking spray, wipe a smear of olive oil or sunflower oil around the insides of the slow cooker. You want a minimal amount – just enough to stop the pizza from sticking.

2. Roll out your pizza dough and press it into the base of the slow cooker evenly. You want the base of the slow cooker to be completely covered and the dough to be as flat and even as possible. This will ensure that it cooks well, so it's worth taking a bit of time to get this right. It should reach all the edges of the cooker.

3. Decant your pizza sauce into a bowl or cup and then spoon it onto the pizza base. Spread it around, leaving a small amount of dough uncovered at the edges to form the crust.

4. Chop your pepperoni and grate your cheese. Sprinkle them across the pizza (or add other toppings if you prefer), with the cheese being the last topping to add so that it covers the others.

5. Put the lid on the slow cooker, turn it on to low, and cook for 3-4 hours, until the crust has turned a rich gold, and the cheese has all melted. Take the lid off and check that you are pleased with the feel of the crust, and then turn the slow cooker off and let the pizza cool in the base of the cooker for 5 minutes (with the lid off).

6. Use a spatula to lift the pizza out of the bottom, being careful not to burn yourself. Garnish with your freshly chopped parsley or any other herbs you prefer, and then slice and serve.

Nutritional info:

Calories: 993

Fat: 65.4 g

Cholesterol: 49 mg

Sodium: 1721 mg

Carbohydrates: 74.9 g

Fibre: 6.5 g

Protein: 27 g

Cheesy Potato Bake

If potatoes are your go-to comfort food, the great news is that these are easy to make in your slow cooker, and this recipe is a real winner, especially in winter. It's the perfect hot meal, and you can always throw in a few other veggies if anything particularly takes your fancy, so don't be afraid to reimagine this dish any way that you want to. Remember, though, that some soft veggies should be added towards the end of the cooking process, so that they don't get over-cooked.

Serves: 6

You will need:

- 910 g / 2 lb. baby potatoes (halved)

- 4 cloves of garlic (sliced thin)

- 1 tablespoon of paprika

- Salt and pepper to taste

- 360 g / 3 cups of cheddar (grated)

- Cooking spray

- 50 g / ½ cup of spring onions / green onions

- 50 g / ¼ cup of sour cream

Method:

1. Line your slow cooker with foil and lightly spray it with cooking spray. This prevents the potatoes from getting overcooked or from sticking.

2. Wash and halve your baby potatoes (no need to peel). If you have any particularly large potatoes, cut them into quarters instead, or they will take too long to cook. Your potato pieces should ideally all be approximately the same size so that they cook at roughly the same rate.

3. Slice the garlic and chop the onions.

4. Tip half of the potatoes into the slow cooker, followed by about a third of the cheddar, half of the onions, half of the paprika, and half of the garlic. Season this layer, and then tip the rest of the ingredients in on top. Reserve any remaining cheddar and onions for the final step.

5. Put the lid on and cook on high. The cooking time will depend on how large the potatoes are, but it should be between 5 and 6 hours, so check it after 5 hours.

6. Once the potatoes are soft, scoop out servings, sprinkle with the last of the cheddar and any remaining spring onions / green onions, and then drizzle a little sour cream across the top of each meal. Enjoy!

Nutritional info:

Calories: 213

Fat: 6.1 g

Cholesterol: 16 mg

Sodium: 395 mg

Carbohydrates: 22.2 g

Fibre: 4.5 g

Protein: 18.4 g

Vegetarian Tortilla Lasagna

If you fancy some tortillas but you aren't sure what to cook with them, how about some tortilla lasagna? You can make this with meat if you prefer, but the vegetable version is delicious and perfect if you're getting into the meat-free world. There's plenty of flavour, and you can make adjustments to the ingredients if you want more vegetables in there to bump up the healthy aspect.

Serves: 8

You will need:

- 410 g / 14 ½ oz tinned diced tomatoes (if you want some extra flavour, choose ones with basil or garlic)

- ½ teaspoon of cumin (ground)

- 3 tortillas

- 170 g / 6 oz of tomato paste

- 880 g / 31 oz of tinned hominy (drained and rinsed; you can use other beans if you prefer)

- 45 g / ¼ cup of olives (sliced)

- 425 g / 15 oz of tinned black beans (drained and rinsed)

- 250 g / 1 cup of chunky salsa

- 240 g / 2 cups of Monterey Jack cheese (or a substitute cheese that you enjoy)

Method:

1. You need to create a grid for your slow cooker using aluminium foil for this recipe. Take three strips of foil and cross them over each other to form a grid that you can place in your slow cooker, going up the sides. This will prevent the tortillas from touching the bottom or edges of the slow cooker, where they might burn. It will also make it easier to lift out at the end. Lightly spray the strips of foil with cooking spray to prevent sticking.

2. Take out a large mixing bowl and add the tomato paste, the salsa, the cumin, and the tinned tomatoes. Stir in your rinsed and drained hominy and black beans.

3. Place a tortilla in the slow cooker, on top of the grid that you have made. It should be supported by the foil strips.

4. Add your tomato and bean mixture, and then a sprinkling of grated cheese. Top it with a second tortilla, and then add another layer of tomato, and another layer of cheese. Put on a third tortilla, and a third layer of fillings.

5. Chop your olives and sprinkle them across the top, and then put the lid on the slow cooker.

6. Cook for 3 and a half hours, and check whether it is hot throughout.

7. Take hold of the foil edges and lift your tortilla lasagna out of the slow cooker. It will be hot, so be careful not to burn yourself. Allow it to stand for a few minutes, and then cut it into sections and enjoy.

Nutritional info:

Calories: 426

Fat: 11.3 g

Cholesterol: 25 mg

Sodium: 644 mg

Carbohydrates: 61.3 g

Fibre: 13.5 g

Protein: 22.5 g

Amazing Slow Cooker Dinner Recipes

Of course, dinner is the time when your slow cooker truly comes into its own. Get some amazing dinner recipes bubbling away while you're out at work, and you'll soon find that you're eating healthier and reducing the temptation of takeaways and microwave meals after work. You simply need to throw the ingredients together before you leave, set a timer (if necessary), and you can come home to a delicious meal with minimal clean-up. This is the perfect way to make yourself eat better and cut back on your food budget.

Beef And Broccoli

If you're a big fan of beef and broccoli from your favourite takeaway, you'll be pleased to learn that it's perfectly possible to recreate this amazing recipe yourself at home. You can make adjustments so that it tastes exactly as you like it, and it doesn't take a lot of prep work, so it's great for an easy weekday meal. You can even take the leftovers to work with you the following day!

This recipe takes about 4 hours to cook, so it's something you may want to set going on your lunch break if possible.

Serves: 5

You will need:

- 680 g / 1½ lb. sirloin steak (sliced thin)

- 120 ml / ½ cup of soy sauce

- 235 ml / 1 cup of beef broth

- 3 tablespoons of sesame oil

- 4 cloves of garlic (minced)

- 1 tablespoon of sriracha

- 100 g / ½ cup of brown sugar

- 140 / 2 cups of broccoli florets

- 2 tablespoons of cornflour / cornstarch

- 4 spring onions / green onions (sliced thinly)

Note: you may also want to cook some rice to go with this meal, but this is optional and should be done separately.

Method:

1. Warm your slow cooker and then add the steak to it.

2. Pour in the soy sauce, sesame oil, sriracha, beef broth, and brown sugar.

3. Dice the spring onions / green onions and mince the garlic.

4. Add the garlic and most of the onions, reserving a few for garnishing later.

5. Put the lid on and turn the slow cooker to low. Cook until the beef is tender (up to 4 hours).

6. Check that the beef is cooked, and then spoon a little of the broth into a bowl and whisk it with cornflour / cornstarch.

7. Pour the mix back into the slow cooker and toss it with the beef, and then add your raw broccoli florets.

8. Mix, put the lid back on, and cook for another 20 minutes. Check that the broccoli florets are tender, and then serve with a garnish of spring onions / green onions. Add rice if you choose.

Nutritional info:

Calories: 436

Fat: 17.1 g

Cholesterol: 122 mg

Sodium: 1719 mg

Carbohydrates: 24 g

Fibre: 1.5 g

Protein: 45.3 g

Slow Cooker Spaghetti Bolognese

There's no recipe that beats spaghetti bolognese for a delicious, rich, satisfying supper, and being able to cook it in your slow cooker just makes it so much better. Tomato sauces benefit from long, slow cooking because it brings out the flavours, and if you haven't usually got time for this in your busy schedule, you'll love the slow cooker version of this classic meal!

Serves: 8

You will need:

- ♦ 2 onions (finely chopped)
- ♦ 1 kg / 2 lb. of lean ground beef
- ♦ 1 tablespoon of olive oil
- ♦ 120 ml / ½ cup of red wine
- ♦ 240 ml / 1 cup of beef stock
- ♦ 1 teaspoon of sugar
- ♦ 2 teaspoons of dried basil
- ♦ 2 teaspoons of dried oregano
- ♦ 2 teaspoons of salt
- ♦ 1 tablespoon of stock powder
- ♦ 6 tablespoons of tomato paste
- ♦ 4 cloves of garlic (minced)
- ♦ 1.5 kg / 56 oz of crushed tinned tomatoes
- ♦ 1 large carrot
- ♦ 500 g / 17 oz of dry spaghetti

Method:

1. Place a large skillet over a medium heat, and warm some oil in it while you peel and chop your onions and garlic.

2. Toss the onions into the pan and gently fry until they turn soft, and then add the garlic and fry for another 30 seconds.

3. Add the beef and break it up with a wooden spoon, stirring until it is starting to gently brown, but no more (usually up to 3 minutes).

4. Tip everything into the slow cooker vessel and put the skillet back on the stove.

5. Add the wine to the skillet and scrape any scraps of beef into the wine. Gently increase the heat until the wine starts to simmer, and then tip this into the slow cooker vessel too, on top of the beef, onions, and garlic.

6. Wash and chop your carrot, and then tip it into your slow cooker vessel. Add the beef stock, crushed tomatoes, stock powder, tomato paste, basil, salt, oregano, sugar, and pepper, and then cover with a lid and turn the slow cooker onto low. Cook for around 6 or 7 hours, or turn it up to high and cook for around 3 or 4 hours if you are in a hurry. Taste the sauce to check that you are satisfied with the flavour before serving it.

7. When there are around 15 minutes of cook time left, boil your spaghetti, following the instructions on the packet, and then reserve 120 ml / ½ cup of the water and drain the pasta.

8. Put the pasta into the slow cooker and add the reserved water, stirring slowly. The starchy water will help to thicken and enrich the sauce. Stir the pasta throughout the bolognese and then serve with grated Parmesan or cheddar cheese, depending on your preferences. You can also add a swirl of sour cream for a richer flavour.

Nutritional info:

Calories: 515

Fat: 10.5 g

Cholesterol: 145 mg

Sodium: 828 mg

Carbohydrates: 52.5 g

Fibre: 3.5 g

Protein: 44.9 g

Slow Cooked Lemon And Salmon

If you love cooked fish, you'll find this melt-in-the-mouth salmon with fresh lemon juice absolutely delicious. It's a filling meal for the end of the day, especially if you serve it with some boiled baby potatoes or a bit of steamed broccoli or some peas. Left to bake in your slow cooker all day, the salmon will become beautifully tender, absorbing all the lemony goodness.

Serves: 4

You will need:

♦ 910 g / 2 lb. salmon fillets (with the skin still on)

♦ The juice from one lemon

♦ 1 sliced lemon

♦ 350 ml / 1 ½ cups of vegetable broth

♦ Salt and pepper to taste

You may also want to garnish your salmon with a herb of your choice, such as parsley, chives, or dill, once it is fully cooked.

Method:

1. If you are using frozen salmon, first thoroughly defrost the salmon in the fridge (take it out of the freezer the night before) so you aren't putting frozen fish in your slow cooker. Frozen foods can mess up the timing necessary for slow cooking properly, and can increase the risk of food poisoning, because they will lower the temperature of the slow cooker and prevent it from getting hot fast enough to be safe. Always thaw foods before you put them in the slow cooker.

2. Take a large sheet of parchment paper and use it to line your slow cooker.

3. Wash and slice your lemon into thin slices, and layer them over the bottom of the slow cooker.

4. Place your salmon pieces on top of the lemon slices in a single layer, leaving the skins on. The skins will help to keep the salmon juicy and tender, so don't remove them before cooking. The skins are edible, but if you would prefer not to eat them, you can simply peel them off before you eat.

5. Season the salmon with salt and pepper.

6. Pour your lemon juice and vegetable broth over the salmon, and check that you have enough liquid. The salmon should be approximately half covered in juice.

7. Put the lid on the slow cooker and turn it on to the low setting. Cook for 2 hours, or until the fish is pale pink and has turned flaky. Take the lid off and check that the salmon is cooked through; it should have an internal temperature of 50 degrees C / 125 degrees F. It is then ready to eat.

8. Lift the salmon out of the slow cooker and place it on plates, with any side dish that you wish to accompany it with. Remove the skins before serving if you prefer.

Slow Cooker Sweet Potatoes Wedges

If you're a fan of simple foods, you might love this vegan slow cooker option – sweet potatoes in your slow cooker. These are supremely easy to make, but still taste delicious and will leave you feeling full and satisfied. You can top them with vegan cheese, or if you aren't vegan, add butter and cottage cheese. If you fancy something more complicated, make a salad or some roasted vegetables.

Serves: 5

You will need:

♦ 1.3 kg / 3 lb. sweet potatoes
♦ ¼ teaspoon of nutmeg
♦ 240 ml / 1 cup of orange juice
♦ 1 teaspoon of cinnamon
♦ 2 tablespoons of brown sugar
♦ ¼ teaspoon of salt
♦ 55 g / ¼ cup of melted butter

Method:

1. Scrub your sweet potatoes thoroughly as you will be leaving the skins on. Rinse them and dry them, and then place them on a chopping board and cut them lengthwise into wedges. You will need a sharp knife, as sweet potatoes can be hard to cut.

2. Once you have the wedges, place them in the slow cooker. Melt the butter in the microwave and mix it with the orange juice, and then pour this over the top of the wedges.

3. Add the sugar, nutmeg, salt, and cinnamon, and then stir the sweet potatoes around to coat them thoroughly.

4. Put the lid on and put the slow cooker on low, and cook for 6-7 hours (do not remove the lid until 6 hours have passed). Test with a fork for tenderness, and serve when the potatoes are soft. If you want to speed this meal up, cook it on high for around 4 hours.

5. Serve hot, with a meat or fish main, or with a dip or sauce.

Slow Cooker Ratatouille

Another healthy vegan meal that's delightfully warming and delicious, slow cooker ratatouille is wonderful when it has been simmered for a good long while. It's also a great way to pack in some vegetables and ensure that you're getting everything you need from your diet, and it's low in fat, so it's perfect for healthy eating.

Serves: 6

You will need:

- 2 tablespoons of olive oil

- 3 garlic cloves (minced)

- 1 red onion (chopped)

- 6 tomatoes (chopped)

- 1 teaspoon of brown sugar

- 1 tablespoon of tomato puree

- 2 teaspoons of thyme

- 2 teaspoons of basil

- 400 g / 14 oz of tinned tomatoes

- 3 red, green, or orange peppers

- 2 aubergines / eggplants

- 3 courgettes / zucchinis

- 1 tablespoon of red wine vinegar

Method:

1. Place a large skillet over a medium heat and gently warm the oil. Peel and chop the onions and mince the garlic.

2. Fry the onions until they are translucent (about 8 minutes) and then add the garlic and fry for another minute.

3. Wash and chop the aubergines / eggplants and add them to the pan, and then turn up the heat and fry for 5 minutes until the vegetables are turning golden.

4. Wash and chop the courgettes / zucchinis and peppers, and add them to the pan. Fry for 5 more minutes, stirring regularly, until the vegetables are all soft.

5. Add the tomato puree and chop the fresh tomatoes and add them too.

6. Next, add the canned tomatoes, the herbs, the sugar and salt, and the wine vinegar, and bring the whole mixture to the boil.

7. Tip the boiling mixture into the slow cooker, put on the lid, and turn it on to low. Cook for around 5 or 6 hours, until all the vegetables are soft and the sauce has turned thick and rich.

8. Serve hot with rice or bread or noodles.

Nutritional info:

Calories: 178

Fat: 5.8

Cholesterol: 0 mg

Sodium: 29 mg

Carbohydrates: 31.2 g

Fibre: 11.9 g

Protein: 6.1 g

Slow Cooker Pork Roast

Pork roasts are one of the most traditional and luxurious dishes out there, and if you love making pork roast but you don't love how much energy this meal takes to cook, why not try this recipe? You'll get rich, succulent pork every time – so say goodbye to dried out meat and the challenge of timing it. Pork turns extremely tender and juicy when it's cooked slowly like this, and you'll probably find that you don't ever want to make a roast the traditional way again! Note that this recipe is a little more hands-on than many other slow cooker options, but it's worth the extra work.

Serves: 4

You will need:

- 1.3 kg / 3lb of pork loin

- 1 red onion (sliced)

- 65 g / 1/3 cup of brown sugar

- 120 ml / ½ cup of water

- 60 ml / ¼ cup of balsamic vinegar

- 2 cloves of garlic (minced)

- 2 tablespoons of olive oil (extra virgin)

- 2 tablespoons of soy sauce

- Salt and pepper to taste

Method:

1. Place a large skillet over a medium heat and warm the oil.

2. Season the pork and sear on each side for about 3 minutes, until it is golden all over. This sear helps to trap the juices in and adds to the flavour of the meat, so don't skip this step; it will make all the difference to the finished product!

3. Peel and slice the onion into thin slices. Layer them around the base of the slow cooker vessel.

4. Put the pork loin on top of the onions and then cover with a lid. You can then choose your cooking time. On low, it will take around 6 hours, whereas on high, it will be done in 2 or 3 hours. This depends a bit on the size of the pork loin, but use this as a guide.

5. When the pork has just over an hour of cooking time left, it's time to make the glaze. Place a small saucepan over a medium heat.

6. Add water, vinegar, brown sugar, minced garlic, and soy sauce and whisk them thoroughly to combine. Bring the mixture to a boil and season it, and then turn it down and leave it to simmer for around 10 minutes so that it thickens and becomes syrupy.

7. Use a brush to spread the glaze on the pork every 20 minutes during its last cooking hour. This will help the glaze to soak into the meat, infusing it with flavour and juices.

8. When the pork is done, check it has reached an internal temperature of 62 degrees C / 145 degrees F (as a minimum) and then stand it on the side.

9. Slice and then serve with your choice of side dishes or vegetables.

Nutritional info:

Calories: 951

Fat: 54.4 g

Cholesterol: 272 mg

Sodium: 707 mg

Carbohydrates: 15.9 g

Fibre: 0.7 g

Protein: 93.9 g

Stuffed Peppers In The Slow Cooker

Stuffed peppers are a fantastic meal because you can pack anything you like into them, and the great news is that they are easy to make in your slow cooker. They're also a healthy option if you are trying to cut back on carbohydrates or wheat products, because they don't involve pasta, rice, bread, oats, or anything else – just vegetable goodness, herbs and spices, and meat. You can make this recipe vegetarian by swapping the ground beef for any vegetarian mince, or using brown lentils instead if you prefer. Skip the cheese and sour cream and you'll also have a vegan meal!

Serves: 4

You will need:

- 450 g / 1 lb. ground beef

- 240 g / 2 cups of Monterey Jack cheese (grated, use another cheese if you prefer)

- 175 g / 1 cup of cooked white rice

- 425 g / 15 oz can of black beans (rinsed and drained)

- 425 g / 15 oz diced canned tomatoes (drained)

- 1 teaspoon of ground cumin

- 1 teaspoon of chilli powder

- 1/2 teaspoon of oregano

- 160 g / 1 cup of frozen corn (defrosted)

- 4 peppers

- 1/2 teaspoon of garlic powder (or a fresh clove minced)

- Salt and pepper to taste

- 1 tablespoon of fresh coriander / cilantro (for garnishing)

- 50 g / 1/4 cup of sour cream (for garnishing)

Method:

1. Take out a large mixing bowl and add half of the cheese, the cooked rice, the beans, the tomatoes, the defrosted corn, the beef, the garlic powder, the chilli powder, the cumin, and the oregano to it. Stir thoroughly so that all the ingredients are mixed together, and season with salt and pepper if you choose to. You can also add other vegetables at this stage if you choose to.

2. Wash the peppers and cut the tops off them. Remove the seeds and rinse the peppers out, and then shake the water out of them.

3. Stuff the beef mixture into the peppers and then place each one carefully in the slow cooker, with the stuffed side up so the stuffing doesn't fall out.

4. Put the lid on and cook the peppers on the high setting for 3 hours.

5. Use a fork to check that the peppers are tender, and then sprinkle the remaining cheese on them and put the lid back on.

6. Give them another 5-10 minutes, waiting for the cheese to melt, and then lift the peppers out of the slow cooker and add a garnish of chopped coriander / cilantro. Swirl a little sour cream across the tops, and serve them hot.

Nutritional info:

Calories: 815

Fat: 28.5 g

Cholesterol: 157 mg

Sodium: 1061 mg

Carbohydrates: 79.4 g

Fibre: 10.4 g

Protein: 61.3 g

Garlic Mushrooms

If you're keen on mushrooms, these garlic mushrooms make a fabulous dish, with a rich and creamy sauce to bring out all the earthy flavours of the mushrooms. The recipe calls for cremini mushrooms, but you can use any you like, provided they are high quality and fresh. If you use large mushrooms, you may need to increase the cooking time, or cut the mushrooms in half to ensure that they cook properly.

Serves: 4

You will need:

- ◆ 4 cloves of garlic (minced)

- ◆ 2 bay leaves

- ◆ 680 g / 24 oz cremini mushrooms

- ◆ 230 ml / 1 cup of vegetable broth

- ◆ Pepper

- ◆ 2 tablespoons of butter

- ◆ 1/2 teaspoon of dried basil

- ◆ 1/2 teaspoon of dried thyme

- ◆ 1/2 teaspoon of dried oregano

- ◆ 60 ml / 1/4 cup of single cream (you can also use milk if you would like a less rich recipe)

- ◆ 2 tablespoons of fresh parsley (chopped)

Method:

1. Wash the mushrooms and chop them if they are large. Peel and mince the garlic.

2. Add the bay leaves, garlic, mushrooms, basil, thyme, and oregano to your slow cooker.

3. Add your vegetable broth and stir well to combine it, and then add pepper to taste.

4. Put the lid on the slow cooker, turn it on to a low heat, and then cook for 3-4 hours. If you want a faster meal, turn it onto high and cook for 1-2 hours.

5. The mushrooms should turn golden and tender. When they have done, mix in the butter and the cream and cook for another 15 minutes. You can also add a little cornflour / cornstarch if you want to thicken the sauce up at this point, but it may not be needed.

6. When the mushrooms are soft and the sauce has thickened, serve the mushrooms into bowls and garnish them with fresh, chopped parsley. You can also sprinkle on a little cheese at this point if you wish.

Nutritional info:

Calories: 132

Fat: 8.1 g

Cholesterol: 21 mg

Sodium: 289 mg

Carbohydrates: 9.2 g

Fibre: 1.3 g

Protein: 6.3 g

Autumnal Vegetable Soup

If you'd like a particularly warming recipe that is packed with vegetables and super easy to make, this one should be ideal. Coming home to a hot bowl of this soup after a long day is delightful, and it's a great way to bump up the healthiness of the meals you eat. This recipe is a good one to toss in the slow cooker before you go to work, because it can be left simmering all day, and it's a vegan and gluten free option (check your stock cubes to ensure they are gluten free if this is important).

You will need:

- 2 teaspoons of apple cider vinegar
- 2 vegan stock cubes
- 3 cloves of garlic (peeled and minced)
- 2 teaspoons of sage
- 3 teaspoons of thyme
- 1 small onion (sliced)
- 75 g / ½ cup of red pepper (diced)
- 130 g / 1 cup of carrots (diced)
- 420 g / 11 cups of squash of your choice (e.g. winter squash, butternut squash, etc.)
- 950 ml / 4 cups of water
- 175 g / 2 cups of Brussels sprouts (shredded)

Method:

1. Peel and chop your onion and mince the garlic. Wash and cut the carrots, red pepper, and squash, and then shred the Brussels sprouts. The smaller you make all of the pieces, the faster they will cook, so if you need the meal quickly, take the time to chop them more finely.

2. Place all of the ingredients except the apple cider vinegar in your slow cooker vessel, and stir them up to ensure they are well mixed.

3. Put the lid on the slow cooker and turn it on low. Cook for 7 hours, and then test the vegetables for tenderness. Choose a hard vegetable, such as a carrot. If they need longer, you can leave this stew bubbling away for up to 9 hours.

4. When the soup is ready, add the apple cider vinegar and stir it in, and then grind in some salt and pepper. Serve piping hot with fresh bread.

Nutritional info:

Calories: 207

Fat: 1.2 g

Cholesterol: 0 mg

Sodium: 341 mg

Carbohydrates: 51 g

Fibre: 9.1 g

Protein: 5.3 g

Conclusion

When it comes to eating healthy with a packed schedule, your slow cooker is your best friend. It will let you make the most out of your food, trapping key nutrients in so that they aren't lost during the cooking process, softening tough meats, and turning vegetables into a medley of flavours and textures. Slow cookers are amazing gadgets, so don't leave your gathering dust in the corner; get it out and let it shine.

You can cook a huge range of foods in a slow cooker, and whatever your favourite recipes may be, there are bound to be ways that you can adapt them so that they can be made over a low heat. If you aren't sure, try researching your top meals online and looking for ways that they can be altered to fit.

Slow cookers can also make side dishes and desserts, as well as things like fresh yoghurt. They have an almost unlimited capacity, so get experimental and start writing out some of your new recipes. No matter what restrictions you have, whether you're gluten free, allergic to shellfish, a die-hard meat eater, or a recent vegan convert, you'll find foods that are perfect for you to enjoy, and you'll also give yourself more free time, away from the hot stove, without sacrificing the quality of the food that you put in your stomach.

More and more people are struggling to find the time to cook, too busy with juggling work, children, and social commitments. On the other hand, with obesity and eating disorders constantly on the rise, and a growing awareness of how important healthy eating is for good health, it's crucial not to be skipping out on vegetables. Finding the time to fulfil cooking obligations alongside all the other tasks of daily life can be a major challenge, and if it's one that you're struggling with, a slow cooker may well prove the answer.

Using a slow cooker and batch cooking for your freezer is a great way to free up some of your time while still making great food for yourself and your family. You can have a whole variety of different meals at your fingertips, and there will usually be plenty leftover to freeze, ready to put in the fridge for lunches or quick dinners when there are other commitments that stop you from cooking.

You may find that it helps to have a meal plan so you know what you're making and when, and to avoid leftovers getting wasted. Make sure you portion leftover meals into airtight containers and put them in the fridge or freezer promptly to reduce the risk of food waste – and ensure that your hard work in cooking doesn't get wasted either. A lot of slow cooking revolves around being organised and planning in advance, which can be a great way to take control of your life and make your kitchen an efficient place to be.

Don't be afraid to try new things with your slow cooker, expanding your repertoire until you have a whole pile of recipes that you and the family enjoy, that you can whip out for any occasion. Learn a few big meals, a few small ones, some vegetarian, vegan, and gluten free recipes, and you'll never find yourself staring at the fridge, wondering what to cook again. Your slow cooker will take over the bulk of the work, freeing up your time to focus on other things and enjoy more of your life!

EXCLUSIVE BONUS

40 Weight Loss Recipes

&

14 Days Meal Plan

Scan the QR-Code and receive
the FREE download:

Disclaimer

This book contains opinions and ideas of the author and is meant to teach the reader informative and helpful knowledge while due care should be taken by the user in the application of the information provided. The instructions and strategies are possibly not right for every reader and there is no guarantee that they work for everyone. Using this book and implementing the information/recipes therein contained is explicitly your own responsibility and risk. This work with all its contents, does not guarantee correctness, completion, quality or correctness of the provided information. Misinformation or misprints cannot be completely eliminated.

Printed in Great Britain
by Amazon